BIRD TAXIDERMY

To

My old friend the late Ernst Flükiger of Interlaken, Switzerland, a Past Master of the Art,

and to

Taxidermists past and present, whose patient and skilful labours in preserving the subjects of Natural History have enriched Science, and have brought pleasure and a knowledge of Nature to many.

BIRD TAXIDERMY

by

James M. Harrison, DSC
MRCS Eng, LRCP Lond, FZS (Sc)

Past Vice-President, British Ornithologists' Union
Past Chairman, British Ornithologists' Club
Vice-President, The Wildfowlers' Association of Great
Britain and Ireland
Member of the Swedish, Norwegian, Danish, Dutch, German and
Spanish Ornithological Societies, etc.

DAVID & CHARLES
Newton Abbot · London · North Pomfret (Vt)

**British Library Cataloguing in Publication
Data**

Harrison, James M.
  Bird taxidermy.
  1. Bird – Collection and preservation
  2. Taxidermy
  I. Title
  579'.4   QL677.7

  ISBN 0–7153–7372–2

First published 1964
Second edition 1976
Second impression 1977
Third impression 1980
Fourth impression 1982

Printed in Great Britain by
Redwood Burn Limited
Trowbridge, Wilts.
for David & Charles (Publishers) Limited
Brunel House Newton Abbot Devon

Published in the United States of America
by David & Charles Inc
North Pomfret Vermont 05053 USA

CONTENTS

ACKNOWLEDGMENTS

The author wishes to make grateful acknowledgments to the following: —

Firstly to Dr. Jeffery Harrison for much helpful criticism and proof-reading etc., to Dr. Pamela Harrison and Mr. E. Fielder for the photographs illustrating this book.

To Dr. David Harrison who proved himself so willing and able in collecting and preparing bird skins for me on his Middle Eastern travels, thus enriching the author's research collection.

To Mr. Reginald Wagstaffe, of the City of Liverpool Museums for information and advice, and to Mr. E. Williams for introducing him to the wire degreasing brush.

He is also much indebted to Miss C. M. F. von Hayek, and Mr. C. de Worms of the British Museum (Natural History, Department of Entomology) for their kind advices.

He also gladly acknowledges the pleasure and help he has had in perusing and quoting from the literature cited (see Bibliography) and he has freely called upon these works in the preparation of this book.

He would particularly acknowledge to Messrs. Macmillan and Co., London, the permission to use the plate illustrating Museum Pests from Dr. Elliott Coues's "Handbook of Field and General Ornithology," and to Mr. Gordon Anckorn for the photograph.

My grateful thanks are also due to Mrs. V. McHugh for typing this work for me from a none too easy manuscript.

JAMES M. HARRISON,
"Bowerwood House,"
St. Botolph's Road,
1st January, 1964
Sevenoaks, Kent.

INTRODUCTION

TAXIDERMY, a word derived from the Greek τάξις, to arrange or fix, and δέρμα, the skin, is believed to be about 400 years old as a practice. Be this as it may, it would appear certain that prehistoric man, when he hunted animals for food, used their pelts in many ways. He may, of course, also have had, or at any rate, may have developed an aesthetic appreciation for the beauty of some of his quarry. This is a fair deduction in view of the mural paintings of the Cro-Magnon cave-dwellers.

This recognition of the intrinsic beauty of natural objects may well have been fostered by the women's innate urge for adornment, and the children's natural interest and curiosity for animals generally. Whether any practical use, other than utilitarian, was made of animal skins is problematical. It is, however, possible to comment that, without a shadow of doubt, the cave-dwellers showed a degree of artistic ability in their murals which would undoubtedly have served them well, had they practised taxidermy. It is equally fair comment to say that during the 400 or more years modern man has practised the art, there has been much inartistic taxidermy perpetrated! The reasons for this are not far to seek, for, for the most part, the operators were uneducated and quite unfamiliar with any aspect of the subjects they practised upon, knowing them neither in life, in the field, nor in the dissecting room as anatomical subjects. Experience in both fields is essential if one aims at doing *good* taxidermy. Moreover, not only were those who practised the art in its infancy ignorant, but they were just doing a job to be

If at first you don't succeed, try, try again.

finished as quickly as possible for the cash paid — no dedication or artistic sensibility.

The earliest attempts at the actual setting up of birds is said to have been made in Holland where a collection of live tropical species had died of asphyxia from the fumes from a stove door carelessly left open. They were skinned, then filled with various spices and subsequently wired in different positions.

Montagu Browne comments upon the background of the evolution of taxidermy as follows: " It must be conceded that to the writings of educated naturalists, who were often medical men, we owe the genesis of the present methods of mounting animals." Amongst these we must mention Sir Hans Sloane, F.R.S. (1660 - 1753), for he bequeathed his entire collection to the nation, and these specimens formed the nucleus of the present collections of the British Museum (Natural History) at South Kensington.

Yet another eminent member of the medical profession to have contributed to the present subject was John Latham, F.R.S. (1740 - 1837), who was in general practice at Dartford ; both he and Hans Sloane lived to very advanced years. Latham executed many bird paintings and prepared bird skins as well as mounted specimens.

Since the volume " The Cabinet Cyclopaedia," " Part I A Treatise on Taxidermy " and " Part II A Bibliography of Zoology with Biographical Sketches of the Principal Authors," 1840, must be amongst the earliest writings on these subjects, William Swainson is deserving of special mention here. The volume itself bears the date as given above, and was published by Longman, Orme, Brown, Green and Longman, and John Taylor, London, though, be it noted that in the autobiography (pp. 338 - 552), there is a note that Part I was printed privately in 1808 in Liverpool. The instructions therein given, considering the date, reflect a most commendable competence: the indisputable scientific approach and responsibility evinced by Swainson is equally apparent. Part II is also an outstanding contribution of contemporary eminent literary and scientific men both bibliographical and biographical.

Of the erstwhile " bird and animal *stuffer*," the last word in this rather invidious description well describes the crude technique from which the modern artistic dermoplastic techniques have evolved. The present day taxidermist is a highly skilled technician, critical to a degree of his own and everyone else's work. In actual fact, the amateur may well claim to have had a profound influence upon the art which, in consequence, later attracted a far better type of professional technician to enter the field.

One may well ask what are the purposes of the practice ? At this point one may again look back and indulge in some reflections, for example, Swainson (1840) remarks of private collections—" They may be classed under two heads: 1. Those intended to illustrate some scientific object. 2. Those formed upon no plan, intended merely for the gratification of the eye." In the Victorian era it was rather the " done thing " to have a few " stuffed " birds in the parlour—this was as true of those dwelling in stately mansions as of the cottagers, but with this difference, whereas the latter had perhaps a pheasant, a golden oriole or a sparrowhawk to show, in the stately mansions there were large cases full of brightly-coloured tropical birds, about which their owners showed a profound ignorance ! The specimens in such cases also lacked any data at all ! These then were to satisfy what is now referred to as " decor." The museums at that time were in this respect badly served and many of the exhibits left much to be desired ; no doubt the technicians there were badly remunerated, whereas the " bird and animal stuffers," of which there were many, flourished and had plenty to do. Fortunately the craze for stuffed birds and animals became less popular, even under the old laws of bird protection ; the man who earned his living by this calling found it unprofitable and many went out of business. A few lingered on, combining taxidermy with other side-lines. With the passing into law of the Protection of Birds Act, 1954, the practice has shrunk to negligible proportions and this makes it easier to outline the true position that taxidermy should hold at the present time. Before doing this, the author would wish to stress some generalities.

Firstly, forming a collection is not for the dilettante who will tire of the pastime. The bearing now of the 1954 Act is particularly to be remembered. Space to house a collection, and the maintenance of such collections must be given proper thought ; under the last two items are the control of museum pests and the inevitable fading of exhibits if kept under ordinary conditions. A deep sense of responsibility enters into this subject, for wild life is not to be wantonly destroyed and a collection of birds, faded beyond recognition and ravaged by moth and beetle, constitutes nothing more or less than an exhibition of what I regard as criminal folly and neglect.

Having given due thought to these matters, particularly in so far as the restrictions imposed by law on the practice are concerned, there is no reason at all why anyone so inclined, should not practise taxidermy to his heart's content, but always remember this—never kill anything without exercising a proper sense of responsibility. However, no bird found freshly dead need ever be wasted.

We may now consider the real purpose of the art. Primarily, of course, it is the preservation of objects of natural history, displaying the intrinsic beauty of the subject as faithfully as possible. Such preparations should be instructive as well as beautiful. To the sportsman-naturalist they represent, of course, a souvenir of " la chasse " as it were, and that may be said to be the limited value of such specimens as already indicated above (see Swainson, *loc. cit.*), except that they may claim an educational value.

The main purpose of the taxidermist's labours must be, of course, to serve science, whether his specimens are destined for a public museum or the museum of a private researcher. No matter for which, let the standard of work be high.

Most museums, both public and private, have exhibition galleries as well as accommodation for cabinet specimens. Here again we quote Swainson (*loc. cit.* III, pp. 84, 85), for commenting upon this he writes, bird skins are above all " the best for scientific purposes. Mounted specimens . . . . occupy a vast deal of room ; they (i.e. skins) can be at all times handled and minutely examined." The latter material is of paramount importance for systematic research in ornithology ; the former, of course, is more for use by the general public who wish to get a general grasp of the different forms of animal life, and the specimens in such galleries serve a high educational purpose. The preparation of specimens for research study is of great importance and the details of preparation presently to be described to produce proper material must be meticulously followed ; badly prepared, soiled " skins " are a constant source of irritation to the researcher. They can indeed sometimes be a sore embarrassment, for when taking measurements, e.g. of the wing, in a badly executed specimen the wing may break off. The slipshod work in which insufficient or no degreasing has been done, will result in the specimen disintegrating completely in 50 or 60 years time. Not so bad, but nevertheless a source of great annoyance and hindrance in routine research, are those specimens so made that to get the required measurements is well nigh impossible.

Master once and for all the correct technique and it will then become second nature. It is unfortunately all too common to find the incision through which a bird has been skinned not even sewn up. A bird skin should be a thing of beauty aesthetically satisfying, as well as made correctly to conform with the requirements of the research worker.

It is the writer's practice to attach, *at the time the bird is skinned*, a small tag label on which are immediately entered the date and locality where the specimen was obtained and also the sex, etc., of the bird.

Badly mounted birds are, of course, intolerable caricatures of birds in life, and are the result of ignorance of the bird in the field and of its anatomy in the work room ; these matters will be discussed presently.

Storage of skins presents less of a problem since the invention of plastics, for the inexpensive plastic bags now available in all sizes provide ideal containers ; these ensure protection against insects, damp and dust, as well as some safeguarding against fading. Also the specimen so contained is air-cushioned from other specimens in the cabinet drawer. Each bag can be closed by one of the various cheap closure devices made for this purpose.

One further point must be stressed ; odd varieties and suspected hybrids, etc., should really be passed on for expert handling, for the scientific value of such specimens cannot, as a rule, be fully assessed from the external characters only. Anatomical and structural modifications are usually present in hybrid individuals and these and odd varieties may, on dissection, prove to be intersexes or sterile individuals or individuals suffering an imbalance of other glands of internal secretion. In such cases the specimens should be sent really fresh, as microscopical and anatomical research is needed in order to resolve the problems they present.

ADDENDUM TO SECOND EDITION

BEFORE his death in 1971, the author left a series of notes in an interleaved copy of *Bird Taxidermy*. These have been extracted for this new edition by his son, Dr Jeffery Harrison.

1. Injection of tarsi and toes with preservative

In the larger species, particularly those with greasy legs and feet such as waterfowl, it is advisable to inject these with a preserving agent, for which a 5% aqueous solution of formalin is excellent. This should be done with a hypodermic syringe, a strong needle being inserted into the ball of the foot. When done in this way, about 5cc of the solution is sufficient to track along the tendon sheaths into the toes and up the tarsus. A further injection can be made into the back of the heel, for which 2cc of solution should be adequate.

2. Decomposition

Some much desired specimen may have to be attempted in spite of early decomposition. This results in the skin tending to 'slip' when handled, carrying away the attached feathering with it. This is most likely to occur below the eye and over the cheeks and abdomen.

Before skinning, the space beneath the cheeks should be injected with a small amount of industrial Methylated Spirit using a hyperdermic syringe. The abdomen should be eviscerated through the usual ventral incision and further spirit should be painted on the inner surface of the skin as it is gently dissected free. Loss of feathering on the face is extremely difficult to conceal, but can sometimes be at least partly remedied by using a purse-string suture with a very fine needle.

3. Cleaning Bird Skins before mounting

The safest method now available is to leave the 'empty' skin soaking for eight hours in a bowl of cold water to which a liquid detergent has been added. This acts both a cleaning and a degreasing agent. After eight hours, the cold tap is allowed to flow freely into the bowl so that the skin rotates as if it was in a washing machine. This washes out all the dirt and dissolved fat with the detergent, which overflows into the sink in which the bowl has been placed.

When the water is quite clean, the skin is removed from the water, which is then gently squeezed from the feathers with some towelling, care being taken not to crush them. The skin is then placed in a suitably large polythene bag with a liberal amount of heavy magnesium carbonate powder. Air is then enclosed in the polythene bag and the skin quite vigorously shaken around inside until it is virtually dry. It is then removed, the powder being shaken out of it, back into the polythene bag. The feathers are then completely fluffed out using a soft brush and an electric hair drier – a task which is best done outside with a long lead on the hair drier and wearing a rubber apron. The powder can be recycled by drying in the oven. The tips of the primary feathers may then need final straightening in steam.

4. Drying

Once mounted, the bird should be left to dry naturally and slowly. No attempt should be made to hasten the process by heating as this can result in the skin drying irregularly, leading to feather displacements.

5. *Polystyrene 'rockwork'*

An industrial insulating material, polystyrene, can be carved to shape, coated with composition and coloured to represent whatever kind of groundwork it is desired to reproduce. This is light and easy to cut and work and is therefore quite the quickest form of 'rockwork' to create. It does not, however, have the strength to support a bird bigger than a duck. A goose, for instance, would require a wooden base to support the leg wires adequately.

6. *Cleaning, degreasing and antimould*

Acetone is an excellent cleaning and degreasing agent and it can be used on birds after they have set hard, when fat subsequently stains the feathers. Being highly inflammatory, it should be used in an open space and an electric hair drier must never be used. Fat dissolved in the acetone must be absorbed in heavy magnesium carbonate powder and the feathers fluffed out with a soft brush.

An antimould, 1% Pentachlorphenol dissolved in acetone is an excellent agent, for the mould is very often associated with underlying fat which is dealt with by the acetone.

7. *Greasy Beaks*

Birds with soft beaks, such as woodcock or duck may sweat grease long after the specimen has dried. If the beak has already been painted, then the paint will peel off. If this happens, all the paint must be removed by wiping over with polycleanse, followed by treatment with acetone, which should be applied once a day for at least ten applications until the beak is completely degreased, before it is repainted.

CHAPTER ONE

SKINNING A BIRD

Preliminary Remarks

BEFORE describing the actual technique of skinning a bird, some preliminary remarks are necessary on various aspects of the collecting and as to the proper care of specimens in the field. All who practise taxidermy and collect birds know full well that the treatment a specimen receives in the field is of the utmost importance. They will also have experienced receiving a bird, blood-stained, mud besmirched and, if in fat condition, also with the feathers saturated with grease and matted together. This brings out the very worst in any taxidermist and increases the work of cleaning the bird enormously. It also evokes invective in the strongest terms. No ; as soon as obtained, plug the gape and vent with absorbent cotton-wool, pushing some up into the cleft in the palate in order to stop any oozing from the nostrils. In birds of prey the crop should be emptied, and water-birds often have a fish, even more than one in the gullet: if not removed, these can cause early putrescence with slipping of the feathers rendering the specimen useless. Also plug any obvious shot holes ; using absorbent wool, gently wipe away any blood on the feathers, and finally wrap the bird in clean paper or put it into a plastic bag of suitable dimensions, and place it carefully in the game bag. These recommendations pay a good dividend.

In fact, it may be said that the proper care of a

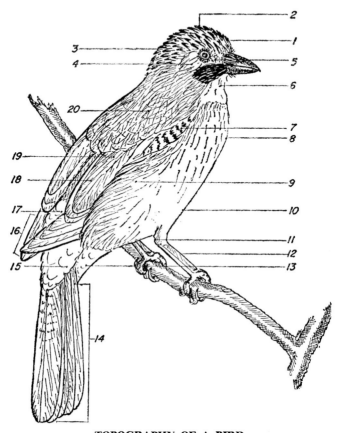

TOPOGRAPHY OF A BIRD

1. Forehead
2. Crown
3. Nape
4. Ear-coverts
5. Lores
6. Throat
7. Wing coverts
8. Breast
9. Flank
10. Belly

11. Heel
12. Tarsus
13. Under tail-coverts
14. Rectrices (Tail Feathers)
15. Upper tail-coverts
16. Remiges (Flight Feathers)
17. Rump
18. Back
19. Secondaries and Scapulars
20. Mantle

specimen commences actually the moment it is picked up! Do not handle it roughly, but pick it up by a leg, or even by its beak when this is feasible. Shake it gently to remove any blood. If sand or dried earth is to hand, this can be sprinkled on as an absorbent. If the bird has fallen into soft mud as often happens to waders and wildfowl then, holding it by the beak, wash the mud off by pulling it through the water until clean. Let it dry out a bit before wrapping it up and putting it into the bag. In all cases keep the blow-flies away. If the eyes are shot through, they must be plugged with absorbent wool. It is always a good plan not to wrap the specimen immediately; this allows body fluids to congeal, and the specimen is less likely to ooze. If these precautions have not been carried out, then the specimen will have to be cleaned by the methods presently to be described. Also birds should not be kept so long as to invite decomposition and consequent " slipping," i.e. loss of feathers. The ideal time to skin the specimen is immediately following the state of rigor mortis. Body fluids have by then congealed and the risk of soiling during the operation of skinning is largely obviated. Birds found dead are all too often already decomposed, but depending, of course, upon the degree of decomposition, can often be salvaged by special care in preparation ; they are, however, usually a gamble and rarely make first-class skins. Nevertheless some experience in dealing with such cases is desirable (see pp. 27-29).

Tools and the Taxidermist

It will perhaps be best to consider firstly what are the absolute " musts " for skinning birds. The requirements are relatively few, but let them be good, although tools

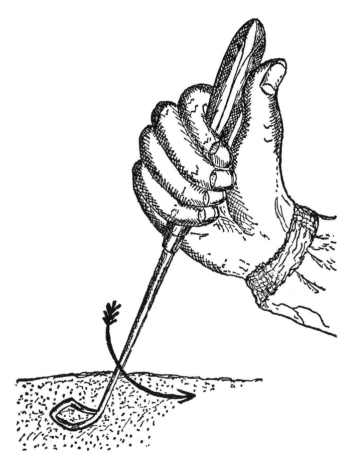

The taxidermical grip of the adenoid curette.

do not make a taxidermist any more than paints and paint brushes make an artist.

Each will decide for himself and choose what appeal as extras. Basically three sizes of scalpels will be needed, one small, one medium and a large. The writer has a decided preference for solid forged surgical scalpels, rather than for the razor-bladed type, of which various shapes and sizes are made to attach to the handle. If it is likely that really large subjects are to be done, then a stout knife, such as is used for autopsy work, should be added. One or two pairs of sharp-pointed scissors and for cutting through heavy bones, ordinary tin-shears, secateurs, one small and one large pair are admirable. Dissecting forceps, but not toothed, are essential. Certain degreasing tools are definite " musts." These include the type of scraper or shaver which can be obtained in any tool shop, but all the corners must be rounded, not pointed. A wire brush such as is used in the Leicester Museum serves the purpose admirably, and to go with it, a small dog comb to clean it up ; in addition a full-bladed large scalpel, which should not be too sharp, often helps, while an adenoid curette is a splendid tool and for degreasing the smaller ducks, etc., is even of greater use than the wire brush. Added to these, needles come into the category of essentials ; the ordinary household type are entirely adequate, but some large half-circle surgical needles are excellent for big birds. A hone for sharpening scalpels is definitely most desirable. It is surprising, however, just what can be done with a pair of nail scissors and a penknife !

It is necessary to pierce the tarsi (scaley part of the bird's legs) in all birds of any size, and for this purpose electricians' screw-drivers with the ends filed into sharp points, in one or two sizes, function admirably. In large birds the pad on the soles of toes at their origin should be incised and with a hook some of the tendons should be drawn out. Although perhaps not in the category of essentials, an ordinary butcher's meat hook, and a set of dissecting chains and hooks can prove most useful to suspend birds when being skinned. This is only occasionally necessary in the writer's experience except in the case of large birds.

For collecting in hot climates where temporary measures become necessary by injecting with the formalinphenol solution (Chapter Three, I, 4), it is, of course, essential to take syringes. The type recommended are known to the medical profession as " Disposable Syringes." These excellent instruments are made in plastic and are therefore unbreakable, one of 2 ml. and another of 5 ml. capacity with suitable needles are recommended. These can also be used to inject preservative into areas which are difficult to skin out, e.g. the wrist and hand segments of the wings and, of course, also the tarsi and toes.

The additional tools needed for mounting birds will be mentioned in that chapter dealing with the technique of setting up.

A word about the working bench as this is important. Firstly you must have good light, both day-light and in order to continue when this fails, artificial light. The latter is best provided by fluorescent tubular lighting ; at times you will be obliged to work late !

The bench must be solid and of a non-absorbent wood which will be improved by a rub over periodically with silicone wax.

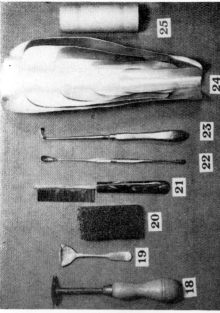

Photo: *E. Fielder*

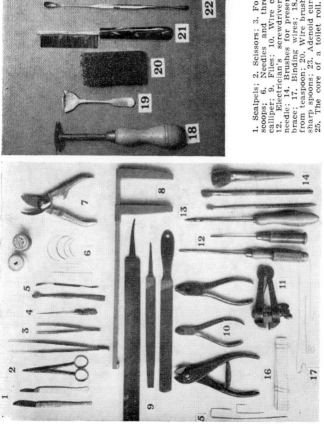

Photo: *Pamela Harrison*

1. Scalpels; 2. Scissors; 3. Forceps; 4. Mounted needle; 5. Brain scoops; 6. Needles and thread; 7. Secateurs; 8. Measuring calliper; 9. Files; 10. Wire cutters and pliers; 11. Hand vice; 12. Electrician's screwdrivers; 13. Heavy mounted packing needle; 14. Brushes for preservative; 15. Wing staples; 16. Tail brace; 17. Binding wires; 18. Scraper; 19. Scraper constructed from teaspoon; 20. Wire brush; 21. Dog comb; 22. Double-ended sharp spoons; 23. Adenoid curette; 24. Aluminium setting forms; 25. The core of a toilet roll.

TAXIDERMY TOOLS: (Reproduced from the author's article "Wildfowl Taxidermy," *The Shooting Times*, June 28th, 1957.)

PLATE I

The work-bench : Good light and everything to hand.

PLATE II

It is of great importance that everything, so far as may be possible, is accessible, so that it is unnecessary to keep getting up for various reasons. A comfortable chair to sit on also adds to the important factor of avoiding fatigue. A two-way plug so that light and the hair-dryer can be used at the same time is essential, and a handy water supply also is most desirable.

Tidiness is scarcely possible, but all the same some control should be exercised, and to clear the bench after every major operation goes a long way towards this end. Certainly powder, loose feathers, sawdust and other odds and ends are to be swept up with the brush and dustpan as often as becomes necessary.

The lay-out and appearance of a busy work-bench during the open season for wildfowl is depicted in Plate II. Finally, if you are going to skin a swan, pelican or other large subject, do it in the garden! Also, of course, if you are going to do a subject that is decomposed, then the garden is the place!!

We will now consider the practical procedures of skinning a bird, having taken into account the hints given as to the pre-skinning " toilet " of specimens.

There are various incisions used in skinning, and one may rightly say that one should be selective in the choice one makes. This is a point which I have noticed does not always receive proper attention even from the professional!

The accompanying sketches show diagrammatically those in general use — each has certain advantages and disadvantages. Of all, certainly the mid-keel of sternum to vent is the most facile, but it is the writer's opinion it should never be used for grebes and not often for wildfowl. If used for species which are white and are being

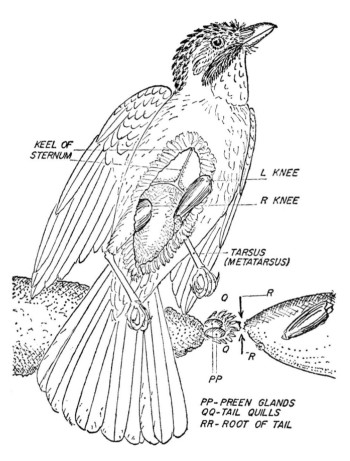

KEEL OF
STERNUM

L KNEE

R KNEE

TARSUS
(METATARSUS)

Q

R

Q

R

PP

PP - PREEN GLANDS
QQ - TAIL QUILLS
RR - ROOT OF TAIL

Mid-sternum to vent incision.

prepared for cabinet skins, and are fat, one may well expect some trouble from fat staining, even when energetic degreasing has been done, for it is very difficult to degrease completely the edges of the line of incision. A good plan is to adopt the surgical procedure which is known as " debridement " in which the edges of the incision are cut away close to the edges before sewing up.

Let us assume, however, that our specimen is outside this category and proceed with the mid-sternum to vent approach. Lay the bird on a clean sheet of paper. If you are right-handed, let the bill point to your left. Now separate the feathers over the breastbone, steady the skin, and with the scalpel start your incision at the mid-point and carry it on to the vent. Note, however, as you make your incision over the abdomen, do so gently, for if you open the abdominal cavity with the enclosed viscera, you will make much trouble for yourself. During the skinning process you should use fine hardwood sawdust liberally to absorb any fluids and so keep the plumage clean. Separate the skin from the body on either side and expose both knee-joints, also loosen the skin at the top end of the incision. Now grasp the tarsus and push upwards until the knee-joint can be cleanly divided. Repeat this process on the other side. Work downwards towards the root of the tail ; when this is *clearly defined*, divide the caudal vertebrae. This is best done by cutting the bones not directly across, but upwards, or in some cases downwards, by a Λ-shaped cut. If cut straight across, there is considerable risk of cutting across the insertions of the tail feathers and they will all fall out ! Three fixed points have now been freed and one can proceed to skin upwards over the back. Presently progress will be halted by the shoulder joints. Thoroughly expose the shoulder joints and divide close to the articulation on each side. Remove any fat you can as you proceed. You will be able to reach the root of the neck with ease once the wings have been detached from the body. At this point some taxidermists prefer to keep the neck attached to the body and proceed to the skinning of the head. The writer prefers to divide the neck close to the body. With the body removed from the skin, do a bit more degreasing. If there are any tears or holes, these should next be neatly repaired on the principle that a stitch in time saves nine ! The preen glands situated on either side of the root of the tail on its upper surface are now to be dissected off. Whenever circumstances dictate, the body can be skinned out by working downwards, cutting through first one wing, then the root of the neck and the other wing, and then the two knee-joints and finally the tail. This order should always be used in the presence of decomposition, and many may well prefer to do so by routine. The leg muscles must now be removed and after that, the wings properly skinned. There is no difficulty at all in removing the flesh from the upper segments of the wings, i.e. covering the humeri, and when doing this, expose by traction and dissection the muscles arising from the next joint, i.e. the elbow, and divide them. If this segment, i.e. the forearm, is not unduly long, it is quite possible to remove all the flesh without undue disturbance and, *under no circumstances* must the attachments of the flight feathers to the larger of the forearm bones (the ulna) be divided. If in birds with long forearms skinning cannot be effected completely from above, then an incision must be made on the under surface, all flesh removed, the skin treated with preservative, chopped tow filled in to replace the muscles and the incision sewed up. The final segments (i.e. wrist and hand, or what is left of these in the bird) are to be incised and preserved. The final segments of the wings can well be preserved by injecting with the syringe sufficient balmex preservative solution or the sodium carbonate-arsenic solution (Chapter Three, I 1, 2 or 3).

The skin is now empty except for the head and neck, and at this point it is necessary to mention that some species of birds require special treatment as the head cannot be made to pass through the skin of the neck when it is turned inside out.

However, we will deal with the ordinary technique first. Replug the gape if this is necessary, then grasp the root of the neck firmly ; this is facilitated by dusting with sawdust to get a non-slip grip. Pull gently and steadily until the base of the skull comes into view. At this point proceed with care: by a combination of dissection and finger pressure, the skin is made to slip over the base of the skull. When the base of the skull has been delivered, you will meet with two checks to progress. This is where the integument dips into the ear-cavities in the skull. In small birds the skin can usually be *gently* pulled out with the aid of dissecting forceps. If, however, this proves not to be possible, then, using the tip of the scalpel, cut into the depressions of the ear cavity until the skin is freed on both sides. It is perhaps worth noting that in snipe and woodcock the ears are situated below the eyes, not behind them.

Your progress will next be interrupted by the eyes, and here special care must be exercised, and the scalpel should be rehoned. Make traction on the skin so as to stretch the attachment to the aperture of the eye on either side. Now with a really sharp blade cut *closely to the eye.* Damage to the eyelids is always difficult to repair. With the eyes freed, continue cutting towards the base of the bill. The skin here is to be reflected until the bases of the nostrils are exposed. Now remove the eyes and the adjacent glands within the orbits. In passing, it should

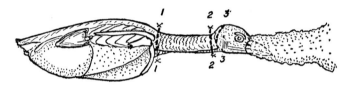

Body skinned out.
1, 2, Division of neck; 3, Removal of back of skull.

Continuation of skull incision. Back of skull, roof of mouth and attached tongue removed.

be noted that with owls, the eyeballs should not be removed; instead with fine sharp-pointed scissors the front of the eye is to be removed and the lens and other contents of the eye evacuated. The cavity is then dried out and painted with preservative, subsequently being filled with white wool. This preserves the forward looking facies, which is so characteristic of owls generally. The brain must now be removed. This is done firstly by cutting closely parallel to the inner sides of the lower jaws within the gape. This step is facilitated by clearing some of the flesh off first. Cut across at the front end dividing part of the hard palate. The ends of these cuts are to be carried on backwards into the braincase to join each other at the top. The back of the skull and the hard palate including the tongue can now be levered out, and any remaining brain cleaned out. This area, and the whole of the head and neck can now be preserved. The empty orbits should be comfortably filled with white wool.

Some birds which require special treatment in skinning the head must now be considered. In this category are the ducks with the exception of some " sawbills," geese, and woodpeckers, with the exception of the green woodpecker and also grebes. In these, it is necessary to make an external incision from the back of the head downwards *over* the nape to the upper end of the neck. Define exactly where the neck joins the base of the skull and carefully insinuate the lower blade of the scissors (or in the case of a large bird, the tin shears) and divide at *this* point. Put in plenty of sawdust and then by traction on the lower end of the divided neck pull it out.

The head is now to be skinned in exactly the same manner as in other birds. Thoroughly clean off all flesh, etc., and preserve. In the cases of ducks, geese and grebes, fill all cavities comfortably with finely chopped tow and sew up neatly. Make sure that the whole skin is now thoroughly preserved and proceed to make it up. The method of doing this varies to some extent as between different operators and in accordance with the species being prepared. We will assume that the subject is a

medium-sized passerine bird. It is the writer's custom
to prepare a suitable stick, and in this connection it is
important to recognise that a bird's neck is not straight,
a fact which must be taken into account, as otherwise
the feathers will not lie as they should at the nape and
beyond. This can be effected easily. The stick is first
sharpened at each end. At the end intended for the head,
cut some shallow nicks to hold sufficient wool securely
twisted on it to fill the cranial cavity, twisting a little
wool to reproduce the natural thickness of the neck, but

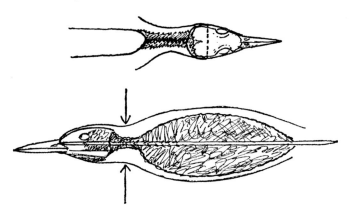

leave the point of the stick uncovered. Leave a little space
and then nick the stick again, twisting more wool on,
moulding this into a fusiform shape—the core of the
body. In practice it will be found best to insert the
sharpened end of the stick firmly into the skull, packing
in wool as necessary to keep it secure and then gently
return the skin of the head and neck with the feathers
right side out. At this point see that the head and neck
are clean and with the mounted needle adjust the skin of

Makes of skin. (Above) Normal form on left, fully crested species on right. (Right) Form to illustrate species with long neck. (Below) Form of skin for long-necked, long-legged species.

Photos: Pamela Harrison

PLATE III

Photo: Pamela Harrison

House-Sparrows (all road casualties).   Mounted by the author.

Photo: Pamela Harrison

Lapwings and Spur-winged Plover. Mounted by the author.

PLATE IV

the eyelids and of the head generally. The gape should be lightly filled with wool and the bill closed by a stitch. If the nostrils are pervious the stitch may be passed through and tied, but in birds with impervious nostrils, push the needle downwards through one nostril, out close to the inner aspect of the lower jaw on the same side and the knot is then tied on that side. Now tie the two upper wing bones (humeri) together at the distance apart which they occupied in life. Do not tie them *at* the joints (elbows), but above this, as otherwise difficulty may well be experienced at a later stage when taking measurements.

The leg bones must next have wool twisted round them to replace the flesh ; a layer of thin wool is laid along the back of the skin and the sharpened lower end of the stick, shaved off rather thin, is made to penetrate the skin in front of the root of the tail. Some additional filling with wool will be required to bring the body up to the correct proportions. This must be done carefully, and when completed to the operator's satisfaction the incision must be neatly sewn up. At the breast the stitches need to be closely approximated, lower down, more widely spaced.

The skin has now to be " arranged "—the bill should point directly forward, the wings are to be neatly folded along the sides of the body, and the legs are to be crossed one over the other and tied where they cross ; they can, with advantage, be tied round the stick. A light criss-cross bandage (surgical open-wove), or a light aluminium setting form with a layer of tow for the skin to lie on, are equally effective for holding the bird while it dries. It is well, during the drying period for skins, to control them to ensure the best results. The time required for skins to

dry is usually inside a week for small birds and up to
a month for large subjects. This, however, depends upon
humidity to some extent.

The technique for larger subjects will now be considered.
In white-breasted birds, in fact I would say in many of
the larger species generally, particularly water birds, the
mid-line ventral incision is contra-indicated and one of
the other approaches is to be preferred. The cut may
be made under the wing and this incision has many

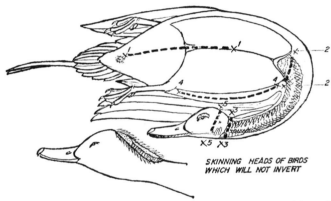

SKINNING HEADS OF BIRDS
WHICH WILL NOT INVERT

Alternative incisions.   1, Mid-sternum to vent ; 2, 3, Division of
neck ; 4, Under the wings ; 5, Removal of back of skull.

advantages, especially for the less-experienced worker.
This incision is the ideal one to use for gulls, terns and
some of the waders, in fact for species which are generally
white or light. When the skin is filled and the wings are
folded to the sides, it is, of course, nicely hidden, but it is
always to be properly sewn up nevertheless. This gives
very satisfactory results. The incision which the writer
prefers, however, especially for wildfowl, is one which

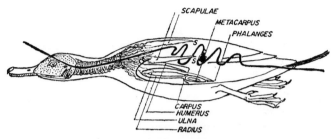

Artificial neck and method of wiring duck skin.

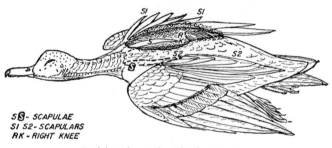

Incision beneath raised scapulars.
(Subscapular)

lies under the scapulars. This approach can be used
whether the specimen is intended for a cabinet skin or for
setting up. In the latter event rather more experience is
demanded of the operator. The great advantage is that the
shoulder-joints and the root of the neck are quickly exposed
and divided, and one then works downwards dividing first
one knee-joint then the root of the tail and lastly the
other knee. It is perhaps desirable to mention again that
when using the mid-keel to vent incision in birds, particularly small birds, which are a bit decomposed, it is
better to skin them from neck and shoulders to knee-joints

to tail root, i.e. from above downwards, and when the abdomen is reached, to apply during the process, a few drops of industrial methylated spirits to fix the feathers by hardening the skin as one goes along.

These larger subjects are to be made up rather differently from small and medium-sized birds and this process we will now describe and we will assume that it is a duck which has been skinned through the incision lying under the scapulars.

With the empty skin before you, as well as the body and neck, proceed to cut a length of suitable gauge galvanised iron wire. The length should be about half as long again as the length of the bird. It is to be sharpened at each end. At about a third of its length from the tail end make a few bends, smaller above and below and widest in the centre. The reason for this is to prevent the wire from rolling. The accompanying figures show how this should be done, and all that is

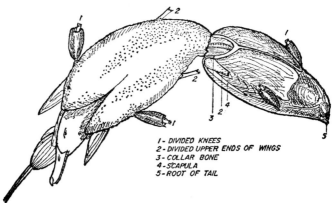

1 - DIVIDED KNEES
2 - DIVIDED UPPER ENDS OF WINGS
3 - COLLAR BONE
4 - SCAPULA
5 - ROOT OF TAIL

The body of duck skinned out by mid-sternum to vent incision.

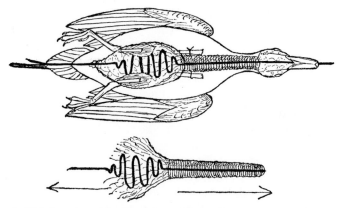

Artificial neck and body wiring. [NOTE: For the sake of clarity the wiring is shown in a bird prepared by the mid-keel of sternum to vent incision.]

necessary at this stage is to make the successive bends fairly close to each other, for reasons which will become apparent presently.

Now with the bird's neck in front of you, make the artificial neck by twisting tow spirally, and always in the same direction, in your hand until firm enough to bind with twine. Several twistings and several bindings will be needed to do this until it is somewhat longer than, but of the same thickness as the bird's neck, and is moreover strong. It should be thicker at the base than at the upper end and it is a good plan to allow the tow at the lower end to fan out.

This done, separate the strands of tow at the lower end and identify the central point of the artificial neck. Taking the long end of the wire, push it up through the artificial neck, but stop before the point penetrates the upper end. At this stage preserve once again the skin of the neck and also the artificial neck itself. This is now to be gently pushed up the neck skin until its upper end can be felt or seen at the back of the skull ; then, and only then, push the wire on until the point can be felt piercing the roof of the skull. The best manoeuvre now is to grasp the wire at its point with pliers and, while controlling the head, pull the wire through. In birds with really heavy skulls the roof can be perforated by an awl to facilitate this step.

Now, laying the skin on its front, open the incision through which the head was skinned and fill round the cheeks and at the back of the head with finely chopped tow and then sew up the incision. This is facilitated by putting the tip of the bill into the jaws of the hand-vice so that the back of the skull is directed and held upright.

[*The description which follows is that for filling a skin prepared through the subscapular incision.*]

Filling of the skin can now be proceeded with ; commence by laying tow over the region of the breast and belly thus cushioning the wire. Since the breast is the most prominent part of a bird's body, there must be enough but not too much there. Having done this and also twisted some tow on the leg bones to the required extent, with a good measure fluffed out above the cut ends of the bones, push the sharpened end of the wire through the skin in front of the root of the tail. Now grasp the end with pliers and pull to adjust the length by opening up the bends as needed.

The next step is to tie the humerus on the side opposite to that on which the incision was made. Gauge the distance apart of the two humeri and knot the two ends of the string at this point. Proceed with the filling of the skin

until satisfied, then tie the second humerus and sew up.
It will be found that the scapulars must be brought level
to those of the other side ; this is done by stitching back
to the top of the incision by a few stitches but not too
tightly, then complete the stitching neatly and meticulously.
Note before sewing up that the two humeri should be
parallel to each other. This filling must be done
systematically and with due regard to avoid both over-
filling and under-filling ; this is a matter of touch and
experience. Do not forget to fill the bill space and throat
with chopped tow. In these larger birds the leg bones
can well be tied together at their upper ends at the correct
distance apart ; this will materially add to the strength
of the skin. Preserve the ultimate ends of the wings and

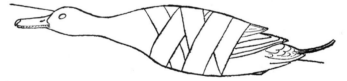

Many-tailed bandage for control of skin.

the tarsi if this has not already been done. It is desirable
to secure the tail feathers between card strips ; they can,
with advantage, be slightly spread.

The specimen must now be arranged for it to dry in
good shape, and it is desirable to have one wing *under*
the flank feathers, the other lying above so that wing
characters can be fully studied on one side, and an
uninterrupted view of the flank provided on the other.

The desired shape can well be achieved by applying
bandages (short lengths according to the size of the bird),

on the surgical many-tailed bandage principle. If an aluminium setting form is used, the specimen should lay on a thin layer of tow, and every few days it should be lying alternately breast uppermost and then back uppermost. Whatever method is used, all skins must be carefully controlled every other day. When the skin is dry, the projecting ends of the wire are to be cut off at either end, taking care not to cut feathers in doing so.

The form of a skin demands a consideration of available cabinet space. Small and average-sized birds can be made with the head and neck directed forwards. Large long-necked birds are not infrequently made with the necks bent, sometimes fully so that the head and neck lie along one side of the body. Such skins are not unpleasing. In very long-legged species it is customary to flex fully both legs at the heel joints, so that the feet point forwards.

The various types of make of skin are shown in Plate III. In fully-crested species, the head is often turned to one side, and some practitioners like to make up owl skins with the face directed forwards, though in doing this the soft feathering of the nape is inclined to suffer during the years, and the writer prefers these species prepared with the bill directed forwards as in most birds.

In making any bird skin there are certain important relationships to be preserved. The first and most important of these is that of the distance between the tip of the wings and the tip of the tail, whether it is the distance from tip of wings to tip of tail beyond, or whether it is the distance the wing tips extend beyond the tail. Bearing on this the " shoulders " (actually the bends of the *wrists*) are to be correctly arranged. The tarsi must be pulled downwards so as to display the heels, and finally no loose feathers are ever to be replaced without a note to this effect, and, of course, NEVER by feathers from any other individual. It is better practice to tie the loose feathers together in a bunch and attach them to the specimen label.

Occasionally a bird will be received which has been packed in a box too small to accommodate it, with consequent bending of tail; this damage, unless the feathers are broken, is easily overcome by holding the tail in the jet of steam from a boiling kettle; the feathers will straighten at once. Similarly, broken feathers can be mended with an adhesive and patience. In large birds the broken feathers can be " imped " as is done in falconry.

The tarsi are to be crossed over each other and tied together where they cross. It is the writer's custom to approximate the feet of larger web-footed birds sole to sole and then tie the toes at two points. The toes are thereby straightened and the taking of accurate measurements thereby greatly facilitated. Bills must be properly closed, as already described and soft bills, as in duck, must not be strongly tied together as this deforms the shape and consequently vitiates the measurements.

It is necessary to mention the preparation of downy young and other nestlings and fledglings. The technique is, in fact, the same as in fully grown birds. However, in the case of very young subjects the skull is soft and collapses completely when the brain is removed. Suitably fine wire should be used instead of a stick and, although the wire can penetrate the skull, a better method is to make a loop at the end of the wire of the shape and diameter of the interior of the skull. Wool is twisted round the wire to reproduce the neck, the loop is inserted into the skull cavity and kept in position by filling with wool. The skin is now to be made up in precisely the same manner as in a grown subject.

Cleaning Bird Skins

Cleaning should be carried out as far as possible prior to making up or mounting. A good rule is to use the simplest measures first ; this, of course, means using plain cold water applied on damp absorbent wool. This is followed by dusting freely with light magnesium carbonate, brushing off with a soft brush and repeating the process. Many blood stains will yield to this process. Shake the skin up with the powder in a polythene bag.

Where fat as well as blood is to be removed then it will be necessary to use petrol, benzene or carbontetrachloride, dusting and repeating as before.

If the specimen is grossly soiled then it will be necessary to immerse it totally in (1) a water and detergent bath until it is clean ; this can be followed by petrol, benzene or carbontetrachloride to remove grease ; rinse well to get rid of the detergent.

It is important that due regard be paid to the precautions indicated in the section dealing with cleaning agents (q.v.).

The cleaning of specimens already made up follows the same principles and processes.

Sexing

All specimens are to be sexed *anatomically*. One cannot rely upon plumage characters for there are at times disturbances of secondary sexual characters giving rise to so called "cocky-hens" as well as "henny-cocks," while there are a number of species in which the plumage of the sexes is similar. An inflexible rule is that unless the sex can be *definitely* determined in this way, it is not to be recorded. The testes and the ovary are the only primary sex characters, and unless the sex glands are seen, positive sexing cannot be noted. It is, nevertheless, useful to make a note of the fact if an oviduct is seen. In most immature birds the plumage tends to resemble that of the female, and the drakes of many species of duck assume a duck-like plumage, the "eclipse" plumage, at the end of the nesting season, when the sexes can be easily confused by anyone insufficiently experienced. Also in southern hemisphere ducks the sexes are similar, i.e. they lack sexual dimorphism.

Sexing is accomplished by exposing the sex glands which lie deeply in the body cavity. In order to do this, the body is to be opened along its left side, cutting through the ribs without damaging the underlying organs. Holding the parts open, gently displace the intestines inwards with the handle of a scalpel. The sex glands (testes in the male, and ovary, sometimes paired, in the female), are situated at the upper ends of the dark-red kidneys. The relationship of these organs is shown diagrammatically in the accompanying sketch (page 26). The sex glands are not to be confused with the small paired yellowish organs—the adrenals, which lie immediately *above* them. If the sex has been properly established, this is to be recorded at once on the small tag label, ♂ for male, ♀ for female. If possible, a sketch of the size of the organs or, if too large, measurements are convincing and valuable.

In very young birds and in the non-breeding season,

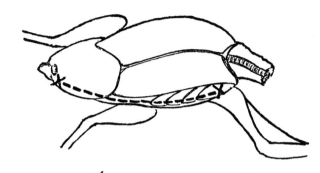

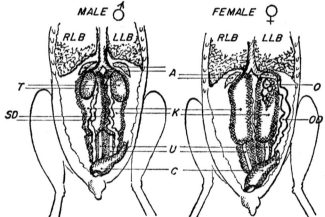

RLB, LLB - RIGHT LUNG .BASE   LEFT LUNG BASE
A - ADRENALS   T-TESTES   K-KIDNEYS   O-OVARY
U-URETERS   C-CLOACA   OD-OVIDUCT
SD - SPERM   DUCTS

Sexing of birds x - - - - x = incision.

the sex glands may be minute and sexing, therefore, is sometimes very difficult or even impossible.

Labelling

The importance of attaching a small tag label at the time of skinning cannot be overstressed ; it is particularly important when there are a number of specimens to be prepared. On it, in brief, should be noted the date, locality and sex, when this can be established ; this represents the basic minimum, and labels, particularly the full data label, should be written legibly and never with a ball-point or pencil, but in Indian ink.

A suitable label measures 3in. x 1in. ; at one end it should be turned over by ½in. and perforated for the thread (preferably crochet cotton) by which it is attached securely to the crossed legs. On one side it should bear the collector's name and a space for an identification number. This side is used to record the name, date, locality and sex, while on the reverse are to be recorded the colours of the eyes, bill, legs and feet and any other relevant data attaching to the specimen. Care is to be taken that all this documentation is neatly written. Slovenly labels with untraceable localities are a serious hindrance to those engaged in systematic work, and specimens with inadequate or vague data are of little scientific value.

While the preparation of decomposing specimens is usually disappointing and uneconomical, some experience in such cases is desirable as, occasionally, a valuable specimen has to be salvaged.

When collecting in hot countries, it is of value to inject specimens in the field and they will then be in considerably better condition to prepare the same evening or even the next day. The solution recommended (Chapter Three, I, 4), is given by hypodermic syringe. The technique advised by the originator of this valuable expedient, Mr. R. W. Wagstaffe of the City of Liverpool Public Museums, is as follows: the fluid is to be injected behind each eye-ball, into the pectoral muscles, into the body cavity on both sides and into the brain case. Push some wool down the gullet and then follow this with the injection fluid administered through a needle of suitable length, but with the point filed off, then plug with non-absorbent wool. The solution is also to be injected up the cloaca which is also to be plugged with non-absorbent wool. If maggots are present, the specimen is to be immersed in benzene. If the specimen has commenced to slip, Mr. Wagstaffe uses a stronger solution of phenol from 10 per cent. upwards in a 1 per cent. solution of formaline with a little glycerine added. When slipping is advanced on the abdomen, this is to be carefully incised in the usual way, the skin gently separated and the area painted with the phenol formaline solution applied on a small brush ; a little alum added also helps. Slipping on the lores and at the base of the bill is best dealt with by injecting on either side within the gape.

In the event of decomposition of such degree that these measures cannot be applied, the specimen can still be preserved as (1) a wet specimen by incising the abdomen, plugging the gape with cotton-wool and immersing the bird in 85 per cent. alcohol, or, if a dry preparation is desired, by (2) injection with 40 per cent. formaline, allowing it to dry when it can be kept as a mummified specimen suitably stored in a plastic bag. If there are no maggots but the skin is slipping, some taxidermists inject widely with a weak solution of mercuric chloride in spirit. Now the burden is temporarily eased by modern refrigeration plants. This allows of some procrastination though it cannot be indefinite.

If birds are to be stored in a deep freeze plant, each should be put into a polythene bag. The larger ones will thus last for up to two years. Smaller birds should be skinned within a year otherwise they become very dessicated and deteriorate rapidly.

It is necessary in passing, to mention that birds found dead may have succumbed to a disease which could possibly be transferable to man ; this is the case with some viral infections. Where this is suspected, special precautions are to be taken. To deal with this fully would demand more space than can be afforded here, and all one can advise is that in any dead bird showing unhealthy signs particularly in the nostrils and gape or with obviously diseased lungs, it would be better for the non-specialist to destroy it by burning and to wash the hands well and use a mild disinfectant.

Taxidermy, when one has a rush on, can be very hard on one's hands, and this is aggravated by the use of various chemicals. Although one does not use them as a routine, the protection afforded by rubber or plastic gloves should be remembered.

CHAPTER TWO

MOUNTING BIRDS

General Principles

IN my preliminary remarks emphasis was laid on an intimate knowledge of birds in the field ; it was also stressed that some knowledge of anatomy is also essential. Field outings and binoculars provide the answer to the first requirement and, for the second there is no better way than to study the plucked body of a domestic fowl, noting the range of movements of the various limbs and in particular the extreme mobility of the head and neck of a bird. This will give a great insight into the relative positions the limbs occupy in various postures when at rest or in movement. By all means go further and learn the more technical side of avian anatomy from the skeleton and a bird's musculature, etc., but as a practical exercise a plucked fowl is ideal.

To sketch in outline the body contour and then super-impose the limbs in action is an equally valuable exercise and a prime first consideration is a correct centre of gravity.

When about to set up a bird it is desirable to have decided in advance upon the posture it is proposed to reproduce, as well as the psychic state of the subject, e.g. whether peacefully at rest, or actively feeding, quarrelsome and excited, preening or about to take off, etc. It is also desirable to decide upon the type of stand, i.e. whether a formal base and perch is to be used or whether

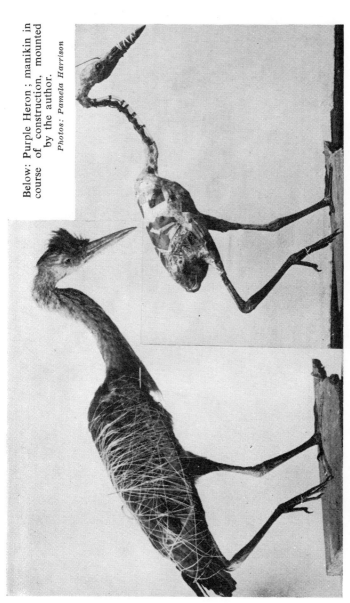

Below: Purple Heron; manikin in course of construction, mounted by the author.

Photos: Pamela Harrison

Left: Same specimen; skin replaced on manikin and binding applied. NOTE: This size of bird could be mounted by the ordinary technique, but was used in order to illustrate this method.

PLATE V

Photo: Pamela Harrison

White-fronted Goose pitching in; showing method of bracing wings
and tail. Mounted by the author.

PLATE VI

these are to approach a natural effect. A formal arrangement, particularly when seen in mass, is far from artistic and should be avoided. An idea of these different styles will be gleaned from examples in the illustrations given. They are intended to demonstrate in one direction simplicity and in the other habitat reproduction. The style selected will necessarily depend to some extent upon available space. In any case when some special character is to be shown, a posture to display this is to be used.

Whenever possible, make the base of the set so that it can, at a later stage, be converted into the finished mount: this is particularly desirable with web-footed birds. A wooden trial stand, bored with many holes of different sizes and variously spaced is very practical: it should be raised by about $\frac{1}{2}$in. to allow the wires to be bent underneath to secure the specimen while work is proceeding. A trial stand for perching birds is readily made, and should consist of a solid, heavy base on to which is stapled a length of wire. The other end of the wire is fixed to a 6 in. length of cylindrical wood of about $\frac{1}{2}$in. diameter. This is variously bored throughout its length. The angle that this perch subtends to the base can be varied widely. Several such trial stands of different sizes can be made to suit specimens of different sizes. Avoid the unnatural artificial branches which are made of tow on wire, glued and covered with lichen, etc.

We can now go back to the point where our specimen has been completely skinned and thoroughly preserved, and needless to say mounting should be proceeded with before the skin dries up. Bird skins can be relaxed but it is always better to mount them fresh whilst still supple. They can be kept sufficiently soft for a day or two if filled with damp cotton-wool and put into a plastic bag, the opening of which is closed, but they must not be left too long.

Wires of suitable gauge and length should now be cut and sharpened ; those for the legs should be heavier than the others. The wire for the head and neck is to be sharpened at both ends, the wires being held in the hand-vice while being sharpened. Those intended for the legs need only be sharpened at one end. The wiring of the wings will be dealt with subsequently. Two wires should be sharpened to support the tail. In the earliest technique the wires were passed for the body and neck and all four limbs, and were then twisted firmly together within the skin to secure stability, the " stuffing " of the bird being loosely done by filling with stuffing pliers. This is only mentioned to be condemned. It is quite impossible to reproduce the natural contours and curves by such a method.

All modern methods employ a firmly made neck and body. The former is best modelled in tow, as already described, for most species. However, it is no bad plan in some long-necked birds, e.g. herons and cranes, etc., to clean and use the actual bony skeleton of the bird's neck, since by so doing, the very characteristic curves and bends can be faithfully reproduced. If this is done, preservative must be applied to the bony neck as well as to the neck skin ; the wire can be passed up the natural bony canal which contained the cervical cord.

The artificial body can be made of various substances, but whatever substance is used must allow of being pierced by the sharpened wires which will support the head and neck and limbs. Peat can be very accurately carved to reproduce the body. The writer, however, prefers to make the manikin of a fine quality wood-wool, binding it and moulding it until an exact replica is produced. Depressions can easily be made by stitching through and through with strong twine on a straight packing needle. It is advisable to cover the wood-wool body thus made with a thin layer of good quality tow and, where there are hollows, these are to be filled in with finely chopped tow, while the root of the tail should be embedded in a mixture of finely powdered pipeclay to which a small amount of dextrin is added and made into a paste by adding water.

The instructions which follow are those for the mounting of most birds, and the modifications required for really large birds will be given subsequently.

In any but the smallest birds, a contour sketch of the body and measurements prior to skinning are, if not essential, at any rate most helpful, although with experience (except for really large subjects) size can often be accurately judged.

Before commencing upon the practical work of making the artificial neck and body, great care will have been spent upon the proper filling of the head. Do not use cotton-wool or your neck wire will not pass. In small birds finely chopped tow is used to fill cavities and a mixture of this and powdered and moistened pipeclay is used for filling the orbits and for setting in the artificial eyes.

In all larger birds the cranial cavity is also to be filled with chopped tow, but the cheeks, etc., are to be remodelled with chopped tow and pipeclay to which a small quantity of dextrin has been added. Some experience is needed in

positioning the glass eyes, or they can be inserted from
without if this becomes neccssary. In owls the glass eyes
are to be positioned on the fronts of the eye-balls prepared
as advised (see p. 12), they are retained in position by
pipeclay and dextrin. Do not forget to fill the throat
or ugly shrinkage will occur.

Having made the artificial neck and body, the former
is to be passed up the skin of the neck in exactly the same
way as in making a bird skin, and the pointed wire can
be made to pierce the skull. This procedure is by and
large the most satisfactory as a better control is afforded in
manipulating the head posture in the final stages. Some
continental technicians, however, having filled the cranial
cavity, transfix the skull from side to side, bend the
wires round the base, twist them together to the required
length and then make the artificial neck subsequently by
twisting the tow, or wool, in small birds, round the wire.
(See Fig., p. 14.)

The artificial neck is now to be securely attached to
the body (see Fig., p. 19). Leg wires, and in large birds
wing wires, must now be passed. In all birds which it
is proposed to mount with the wings at rest, tie the wing
bones together at the correct distance apart, having, of
course, primarily filled the forearm segments with finely
chopped tow to replace the flesh removed ; they can then
be stapled to the side, but in large birds the wings should
be wired as has to be done when the subject is to be
mounted flying. Twist tow on the leg bones to reproduce
the muscles but this must not only be twisted on, but
firmly bound on with twine, to give the specimen stability.
Having filled the space round the root of the tail as
described above, manipulate the body into position and

The manikin and supporting wires *in situ*. Note the tie between the upper wing bones (humeri). For the sake of clarity, wing staples are not shewn.

(Reproduced from the author's article "Wildfowl Taxidermy," *The Shooting Times,* June 28th, 1957.)

proceed to pass the leg and wing wires through the manikin and bend the ends so that they can be securely bolted back into the body. The point of entry of each leg wire will have been determined by the choice of posture, e.g. at rest or in motion. Having sharpened the two tail wires, pass them through the root of the tail and for some distance into the manikin.

Now review the work and, if satisfied with the filling, sew up neatly, keeping the stitch holes near the edges of the skin and taking care that all feathers are free.

The limbs can now be approximately put into position and the specimen wired on to the trial stand. It is at this point that your artistry will be tested and your field experience will be called upon. The wings, if folded, are to be stapled to the body, the plumage being deftly arranged and the chosen posture manipulated, and be sure to see that the tip of wing to tip of tail relationship is correct. The mounted needle and fine forceps, soft brush and digital coaxing all have a place at this stage to produce the desired effect.

View your work from every angle and do not necessarily press every feather down. Keep in mind whatever state and posture you wish to express and arrange the plumage accordingly. An electric hair-dryer can be an inestimable boon! The specimen is now under control in so far that it is standing up or perching in the selected posture, the wings having been secured to the sides, and all that is now needed is to secure the feathers while the bird dries. Firstly attend to the tail: for this purpose cut two strips of card, place one underneath the tail feathers, but above the undertail-coverts, place the other strip on the upper surface, but under the upper tail-coverts. Spread the tail feathers as required and secure both strips of card by using the ordinary slip on paper-clips. The method of securing the tail in large birds is by transfixation of the quills near their bases by means of a sharpened piece of wire.

There are various ways of keeping the plumage in orderly array. It can be done by laying over with narrow strips of damp tissue paper. Another method is to cut strips of fine paper, lay it over the specimen securing it in position by using fine (entomological) pins. The writer has recently used strips of thin polythene for controlling feathers. This is pinned on and has the advantage that the setting of the plumage is under full visual control. The best method, however, in the writer's opinion is the binding method. Cut and sharpen a number of fine wires of about 6 in. in length. At the unsharpened end make a ∽ bend (see Fig., p. 35). These wires are inserted in the midline of the specimen above and below, i.e. along the breast and belly and along the back. Now with a *soft* fine cotton (such as is used for crochet work), proceed to " bind " the bird, arranging the feathers as this is done. Avoid putting tension on the binding, and where no binding is required, leave well alone. It will, however, be found that in young birds when the plumage is loose and soft the binding needs to be of the " cocoon " type in order to get a proper contour effect when this is required. This is illustrated in the mounted full immature and moulting purple heron (Plate V). Of course where the fluffy effect of a young bird is needed, use no binding at all and keep the fluffiness by using a soft camel hair brush until the specimen is dry. When satisfied with this, see that the toes are properly positioned ; they can be kept correct by the use of pins. Great care is to be taken over the eyes. Arrange the eyelids and, especially in larger birds, set them by using very small pledgets of damp cotton-wool held in the fine pointed forceps. When you consider the work finished, put it aside to dry, but control it daily. See that you have a note of the colour of the soft parts with the specimen so that they can be correctly coloured when it is

dry and see also that a small tag label is attached to the
bird bearing its full particulars.

When it is desired to mount birds flying or with the
wings spread, the wing wires, sharpened at both ends,
must be passed along the whole length of the wings.
The wires then transfix the manikin and are bolted back.
The wing bones are not tied together, but the wires should
be tied to the humeri at one or two points. The flight
feathers can be controlled by strips of stiff paper and
pins. Nice judgment is required in suspending flying birds
to get a natural balance and poise. They can be suspended
by very fine wire, or better still fine nylon, from a loop
of wire hidden in the feathers of the back.

Although the average amateur will probably not wish
to prepare large subjects, this book would not be complete
without an account of how this is to be done. All birds
of swan size and over require what is known as a centre-
board. The best technique is as follows: having skinned
the body, lay it on a sheet of brown paper. With chalk,
make an accurate outline sketch by drawing round the
cadaver. This can be pasted on to a piece of ½ in. deal
and is then to be sawn out. Before disposing of the body,
take measurements of the thickest part of it; this is, of
course, over the pectoral muscles and also over the centre
of the abdomen. The measurements should be taken at
measured lengths from the root of the neck. Holes can
be drilled about 1 in. from the edge of the centre-board
at the determined distances, through which wires are passed
to reproduce the thoracic cage and abdomen, but it is
particularly to be noted that these diameters are *not*
circular in form but roughly inverted pear-shaped.

To proceed further, it is necessary to determine the

position of the legs as it is essential to screw to the centre-board blocks to which the leg irons are attached. They should measure across, including the centre-board, the distance on the skinned body between the two hip-joints. Having passed the leg irons and reproduced the leg musculature, the blocks are then to be grooved to accommodate the irons which are secured by small metal plates screwed to the blocks. A similar technique is best employed for large birds for securing the wings.

The stout wire for the head and neck is also screwed securely to the centre-board. To complete the work, filling can be accomplished on the framework provided by centre-board and wires. This should be done systematically and *loose, haphazard " stuffing "* is to be avoided.

There is a further method somewhat akin to the dermoplastic method used for mammals, which utilises the skeleton of the bird as the framework. In this method the skin is completely removed even by cutting it carefully away where it joins the bill. The only other variation in skinning is that when the legs are reached, an incision is made along the inner side of each and the skin is carefully removed leaving the legs attached to the body. The entire skeleton is thus intact, with the exception of the wing bones which are disarticulated at the shoulder joints. From the carcass remove all flesh and eviscerate completely. Wash the skeleton thoroughly in cold water to clean off all blood and scraps. The body cavity is to be filled with a wooden core to which the leg and wing wires and the head and neck wires are to be anchored.

The detached skin with the tail attached, is washed, degreased and preserved with the wings (properly skinned)

and then dried. It is then wrapped in cloths dampened
with a solution of carbolic acid (Chapter Three, I, 7).
These cloths are to be kept damp during the making of
the artificial body. The position it is proposed to reproduce
is to be secured in the skeleton which is then painted with
formaldehyde (Chapter Three, I, 6). Once this is done
it cannot be altered as it will set hard. The next step
is to model the musculature, etc., on the skeleton in
papier-mâché, layer by layer, allowing each to dry before
applying the next, doing a little at a time from measurements taken after skinning. This work must be allowed
to dry thoroughly, a lengthy process in a large bird.
When dry, coat with shellac to waterproof it. It is now
ready to receive the skin which is carefully pulled over
it and secured with pins. The natural colours of the
soft parts are restored by oil paints and the specimen
put on its permanent mounting. A little copal varnish is
to be mixed with the colours, but great care has to be
taken not to use this to excess as the effect produced
will then be most unnatural. A very practical modification
of this method is carried out as follows: the bird is
skinned as has already been described but the legs are
detached. The actual bony neck is utilised.

Prepare a solid wooden block cutting off all the corners.
Its length should be a bit shorter than the length of the
bird's body, its width should equal the distance between
the two hip joints. With wire-netting, make a frame the
shape of the body, staple this to the block. Having
cleaned and preserved the neck skeleton, pass the wire
as already described. Staple this to the upperside of the
block, then bend it to the desired posture. Now having
withdrawn some of the tendons and preserved the tarsi,

pass the leg wires. Determine the leg positions and bend
the wires accordingly. Next bind tow on to reproduce the
flesh. Having done this, staple the leg wires securely to
the block. Now fill the spaces between the block and
the wire-netting shape with tow or fine wood-wool until
a rough approximation to the bird's body is achieved.
The specimen can now be put into the position it is to
be in on a temporary stand (see Plate V).

Next proceed to paste *small*, irregular pieces of news-
sheet to cover all the basic body work including the
legs, but do not treat the neck this way. Build the whole
structure up thoroughly and allow it to dry.

Pierce the vault of the skull and add the head, the
cavity of which is to be filled with wood-wool or tow.
The neck bones and skull are to be painted with
formaldehyde and then the preservative.

The neck is, of course, much too thin, and since the
neck and its structures are, in section not circular but
inverted pear-shaped, its reconstruction must be the same.
The writer's method for doing this can be seen in the
plate showing the unfinished model. Firstly a length of
plastic tubing of the correct diameter is fixed in the
gape, it is then made to follow the sinuous curves of
the neck vertebrae being secured by wire twisted first
round the tube and then round the vertebrae. At its
lower end it is made to dip into the space above the
clavicles (wish-bone).

The next step is to fill the cavities of the skull with
papier-mâché, set in the eyes correctly, viewing from in
front as well as from side to side, and then proceed to
build up the neck using papier-mâché as required.

When the model is thoroughly dry, coat with shellac

for damp-proofing and proceed to drape and arrange the skin, which is held in position by pinning where required. Both the last two processes of mounting are complicated techniques and require a ripe experience.

This method can also be used in making models of extinct species, except, of course, that the skull and bill, legs and feet have to be carved out of balsa wood or modelled in some pliable hard-drying substance. The wings are best constructed of wire. Correct measurements and details of the species that is being reproduced must be obtained from the relevant literature. When the manikin has been constructed and is dry, it has to have feathers pasted on one by one—a long and tedious process, but with infinite patience and careful selection of feathers, good replicas of such species as the great auk and dodo can be achieved.

Quite recently an entirely new technique is on trial and has been described as mounting birds by deep freezing. The specimen to be mounted is wired in position and then subjected to prolonged deep freezing. The long term results of this method will, of course, have to be assessed in the course of time before it can be said that it will supersede the time-honoured and conventional techniques.

It is sometimes desired to relax skins and either remake or even mount the specimen. Much will depend in this process upon the skill with which the bird was orginally prepared. Small birds relax readily. Firstly undo the stitches, take out as much of the filling as is easily withdrawn, then fill with moist wool and place in a box with a tight-fitting lid. The skin can, with advantage lie on dampened wool. Small birds are relaxed in 24 to 48 hours. Skins can be kept moist in plastic bags but all skins undergoing relaxation should be controlled every day, otherwise they can easily spoil. When being worked, a drop or two of glycerine is sometimes helpful, or the American preparation, skin relax, can be used.

The temporary preservation of fat water-birds (also other large birds) can be effected by rubbing in table salt after washing off blood-stains; the salt must be well rubbed in, especially into the wings and around and into the skull cavity. Such skins can then be folded with the skin surfaces in apposition. In this state they will last a long time. Relaxation is effected by immersion in water and washing in running water to remove all the salt. As soon as it can be turned inside out, all fat is to be scraped off after which immerse it in Huber's solution (Chapter Three, II, 5). According to Huber who devised this method, immersion should be for 24 hours and can, with advantage, be repeated for a second similar period. After gently squeezing out, drying is assisted by shaking the skin up in a plastic bag into which light magnesium carbonate has been put. This is best done out of doors when the skin can be shaken and brushed with a soft brush in the open air, always brushing lightly in the direction in which the feathers grow. One must, however, mention that salt, either by itself or in combination with alum, is believed by some authorities to give rise to undesirable colour changes later in the life of the specimen. There are those who consider that the turpentine which is added to restore gloss to the plumage, should be used in far smaller quantities than in Huber's solution.

At times it is necessary to mount birds having combs and wattles. These structures cannot just be allowed to dry not even if preserved by injection treatment; if this is done they will shrivel up and look most unnatural.

They should be cut off cleanly with a razor blade close to their origins: make an outline sketch on paper and then make a mould in plaster of paris of the structures from which a cast can be made. By doing this the wrinkles, creases and warty excrescences are faithfully reproduced. The next step is to cut out of light tin or aluminium foil a slightly smaller copy of the paper outline sketch. The base should be splayed out here and there on either side so that it can be more easily attached to the skull. Now in papier-mâché or other modelling substance, make a positive from the mould. The metal foil is to be incorporated in the papier-mâché positive. This, when dry, is to be fixed in position on the head, finally being correctly coloured. A note of the colour should, of course, be made when the structures are fresh.

It is possible that some readers may wish to make artificial rocks, etc. The construction of such is shown in Plate VIII and is as follows : first, select a suitable base of wood, then from small-mesh wire-netting, shape the rocks you wish to reproduce and see that the model is strong. The wire shape must be stapled on to the base. Having made the wire foundation work, proceed to paste on *small* irregular shaped pieces of newspaper. The secret of this is to keep the pieces *small* and paste one overlapping the other. Ordinary paste can be used and the work must proceed to the point where the underlying wire-mesh is completely hidden. Leave a window at the back so that the specimens can be securely wired on.

The next stage is to coat the whole structure with a composition of glue, plaster of paris, silver sand or grit, smooth or rough, according to the texture of rock it is desired to imitate. Time can be saved if, into this composition, suitable dry colour powders are mixed to provide the ground colour of the rocks desired. When this composition work has dried, to obtain relief effects colour with oil paints. Snow is reproduced by painting the rock-work white and incorporating finely powdered glass, some loosely scattered over the surface enhances the sparkle of the frosty effect. Vegetation can be added to such rock-work but see that its condition is in keeping with the seasonal state of the birds.

Such bird, or bird groups, can be shown in the main display cases, or cased individually according to taste and space. Backgrounds to cases can reproduce the distant countryside, or by the use of shades of distemper, usually sky-blue, yellow and pink, a sky effect can be achieved according to the skill of the worker.

*   *   *

Cases to contain mounted birds can be all glass, except for the base, or glazed in front and on sides. Some favour half-glazed sides and top. Different circumstances will dictate the case to choose for each specimen. For strength, an all-wooden case glazed only in front has much to recommend it.

The glasses are fixed in, according to size, by pasting with paper strips or by wood fillets kept in place by brads in large cases. To blacken wood-work, use lamp-black and glue, finally applying Japan Black to provide a finish.

There is much scope for artistic achievement, but first acquire a proficiency based on observations of the subjects in life, then familiarise yourself with their anatomical build and finally master the various techniques used in modern taxidermy.

Ancillary research

It is most desirable to make the maximum use of all specimens, and when proceeding abroad or even in this country those who collect birds may be asked by interested zoologists to collect endo- and ecto-parasites (worms, flukes, fleas, ticks, mallophaga and hippoboscid flies) or even to prepare simple lung smears for the detection of microfilariae, etc., or maybe the conservationist seeking information on stomach and intestinal contents will ask for the whole digestive tract. The technique of evisceration for this purpose was evolved by Jeffery Harrison. This has perforce to be slightly modified when a bird is being prepared as a museum specimen. The main point is to push cotton-wool down the gullet before skinning in order to push down with it into the stomach any food stuffs that may still be in the gullet. The rest of the operation is ligaturing the gullet above the cotton-wool, plugging the cloaca and ligaturing below the plug. The whole of the digestive tract is then dissected out *en bloc*, labelled with a tag label with pencil and put straight into the formaline solution (Chapter Three, I, 5). In the case of duck, the food plants can be identified and a programme of planting on a sanctuary instituted.

Such requests should, whenever possible, be agreed to, and those making them are always willing to assist by giving details of how to set about the work, and will often provide the simple apparatus required.

It may so happen that in the course of preparing birds an unlaid egg may be discovered. To meet with this

Below: Immature drake Teal, showing method of binding, etc. Mounted by the author.

(Reproduced from the author's article "Wildfowl Taxidermy," *The Shooting Times*, June 28th, 1957.)

Photo: E. Fielder

Photo: Pamela Harrison Left: **Pintail drake alighting. Mounted by Jeffery G. Harrison.**

PLATE VII

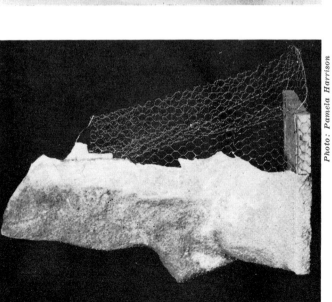

The finished work: House-Martin, Sand-Martin, Swallow and Swifts mounted by the author, Alpine Swift mounted by the late E. Flükiger.

Construction of artificial rock-work using wire netting.

PLATE VIII

contingency an egg drill is desirable. The hole is drilled on one side and the contents are washed out by injecting water into the egg by means of a syringe. If the egg is hard set, a large hole becomes necessary and the embryo has to be cut into small pieces and extracted by a small, fine hook. The data can be neatly written round the hole on the larger eggs but the small ones necessitate a registered code number and entry in a note book.

CHAPTER THREE

MATERIALS

IN this chapter will be found the materials and formulae for solutions, agents, etc., used in the various procedures of taxidermy. It is thought that this will prove a convenience for easy reference. Many of these can be purchased at the hardware and general stores, others need to be bought from drugstores. Care in the use of some of these is an urgent and responsible necessity for they can be dangerous both to the user and others. Although basically, arsenic remains the preservative of choice, other and safer preparations are now available and to these the average amateur is recommended.

I. Preservatives:

1. Sodium arsenate, one ounce.
   Water to, one gallon.

Use: For preserving skins and mounted specimens. For small birds use one part preservative, one part industrial methylated spirit to eight parts of water. For larger subjects increase the strength of preservative and spirit accordingly up to a maximum of $33\frac{1}{3}$ per cent.

Comments: Must be labelled *poison* and kept under proper control. *Wash hands after use.*

2. Atlas preservative.
   Commercial hide preservative (arsenical).
   (Supplied by The Atlas Preservative Co. Ltd., Fraser Road, Erith, Kent.)

Use : As for I, 1.

Comments: As for I, 1. This preservative can only be supplied through an accredited dealer in poisons.

3. Sodium carbonate, 250 G.

    Arsenic, 50 G.

    Water to, one litre.

    Use: For the preservation of animal tissues, e.g. small subjects (whole), organs or parts of organs. Preserves natural colours to some extent.

    Comments: As for I, 1 and 2.

4. Formosaline and phenol.

    Formosaline (formula I, 5), five per cent.

    Phenol, three per cent.

    Use: Injectable preservative for temporarily delaying decomposition.

    Comments: An irritant *poison*, to be kept under proper control.

5. Formosaline.

    Formaldehyde, 10 per cent.

    Normal saline (one teaspoonful of salt to one pint of water), one pint.

    Use: For the preservation of tissues and whole subjects. (Tissues for microscopical study should not exceed one cubic cm., a general fixative when routine microscopical research is contemplated.)

    Comments: As for I, 4.

6. Formaldehyde, 40 per cent.

    Use: For use neat, or diluted as required.

    Comments: A strong irritant, should be labelled *poison* and kept under proper control.

7. Carbolic acid solution.

Carbolic acid, one and a half tablespoonfuls.

Water, one gallon.

Use: For keeping skins dampened while work proceeds on manikin, also in relaxing box.

Comments: Must be labelled *poison* and kept under proper control.

8. Borax preserving solution (non-poisonous).

Powdered borax, four ounces.

Water, one gallon.

The powder to be dissolved in water until a saturated solution is made, i.e. no more will go into solution.

Use: Preservation of skins.

Comments: Its use for moth-proofing is open to question.

9. Industrial methylated spirit.

Use: Can be used to preserve by immersion of subject, useful during skinning of decomposing subjects. As a glass-ware cleaner.

Comments: Keep under proper control, inflammable.

10. Balmex preservative.

Van Dyke, Woonsocket, South Dakota, U.S.A.

Use: For preservation of tarsi, toes and extremities of wings, use by injection technique.

Comments: Avoid contact with hands.

II. Cleaning and Bleaching Agents :

1. Petrol (colourless).

2. Benzene.

Uses: Both substances are excellent cleansing agents, but not for blood-stains. They remove fat and grease.

If used to excess will remove the gloss from the plumage. (See Huber's solution, II. 5). Decomposed specimens can be immersed to kill maggots.

Comments: *Highly inflammable. Do not use in presence of flame, or electric element, or indoors.*

3. Carbontetrachloride.

Use: A highly effective cleanser but is now regarded as liable to give rise to undesirable colour changes in specimens. Excellent for cleansing grease-saturated labels. Has no effect on writing, unless this has been done by ball-point, which incidentally should never, in any case, be used for zoological purposes.

Comments: Do not use this substance indoors ; it is a grievous liver poison. If it is used for long periods in an enclosed space its effects could be very serious. Prolonged inhalation is, it is thought, capable of inducing lung cancer.

4. Detergents.

Uses: There is a very wide choice of these as, domestically, they are in much demand. Any of them can be of great service in cleaning but should be well rinsed out and followed by a benzene bath.

Comments: It is as well to wear plastic gloves when working with these, as a skin rash can result if the user happens to be sensitive.

5. Huber's solution.
    Petrol, two gallons.
    Alcohol (industrial methylated spirit), one pint.
    Spirit of turpentine, four ounces.

Use: A first rate cleanser ; the added turpentine is to restore gloss to the plumage.

Comments: *Do not use indoors, or in the presence of a flame. Must be kept air-tight and not left uncovered.*

6. Hydrogen peroxide, 20 per cent.

Use: A strong bleaching agent ; should not be used on the plumage. Dilute as required.

Comments: *Never fill the bottle to capacity. Keep in a cool, shady place. Liable to explode.*

7. Hypochlorite solutions.

Use: For bleaching bones ; caution, when used for small subjects it must be well diluted and its effects carefully controlled in small specimens otherwise will damage such.

Comments: Should be kept under proper control.

III. Absorbents:

1. Hardwood sawdust.

Use: The best substance for use during skinning operations.

2. Light magnesium carbonate.

Use: To absorb moisture after cleaning operations. It is best to dust the plumage out of doors. Some workers prefer the heavy magnesium carbonate.

3. Potato flour.

Use: As above and can be thoroughly recommended.

4. Plaster of paris.

Uses: This is a useful and cheap substance ; it is inferior to 2 and 3 as being less easily removed from the plumage if used freely. It is also used to make artificial rock-work and moulds for taking casts. There are, of course, numerous other substances which one can use, however, *never* use ordinary flour, as this is quite unsuitable.

IV. Relaxing Adjuvents:

1. Glycerine.

2. Skin relax.
   (Van Dyke, Woonsocket, South Dakota, U.S.A.)
   Comments: Avoid contact with hands.

V. Adhesives:

1. Carpenters' glue.
   Uses: Many, and readily available, cheap.

2. Bonding agents.
   Uses: As for carpenters' glue; there are many proprietary brands — all are excellent but somewhat expensive, they are, nevertheless, time savers and very convenient.

3. Tube adhesives, useful for small jobs, many proprietary brands.

Pastes.
   Uses: These are essential and enter into the construction of artificial rock-work and also artificial bodies by some methods. They are basic in the making of papier-mâché.

4. Flour paste, water (Montagu Browne).
   Flour, 10 ounces by measure (or seven ounces by weight).
   Water, 10 ounces and five ounces by measure.
   Oil of cloves, half ounce.

5. Flour paste, oil (Montagu Browne).
   Flour paste, 10 ounces by measure (or seven ounces by weight).
   Linseed oil, five ounces by measure (or nearly five ounces by weight).

6. Combined pastes (Montagu Browne).

This is used as a pulp in equal proportions.

Flour paste, water, five ounces.

Flour paste, oil, five ounces.

Tissue paper, six sheets.

Its use is principally for making casts: Should be well pressed into the mould, the excess oil being absorbed by wadding during the process.

Note: Excellent flour pastes are obtainable from the photographic stores.

VI. Modelling Substances:

1. Modelling wax (Moyer).

Beeswax, three pints.

Resin, one pint.

It is recommended that only pure white beeswax is used. The two substances are melted separately over a hot-water bath. They are then mixed in the melted state and poured into small moulds until required for use.

2. Papier-mâché.

This is a very important substance and can now be purchased from the taxidermy stores (American).

For those who wish to make their own, the method briefly consists of taking several sheets of tissue paper, pasting them on both sides with flour paste and then beating and pounding them up in a metal mortar, adding some powdered pipeclay, and continuing to work on the mixture until a homogenous mass results.

As a rough guide for those wishing to make their own, take about one ounce of tissue paper, five ounces of thick flour paste and one ounce of powdered pipeclay and pound in mortar as above.

3. Fibre glass paste.

Obtainable from the hardware stores. Is easy to mix and dries extremely hard.

4. Glycerine.

Can be added as a softener of over-stiff modelling pastes. Aids relaxation of skins.

VII. Insect Repellants:

1. Naphthalene.

This substance is sold variously as moth balls or flakes. Is now believed to be the best substance; occasionally gives trouble by vaporisation and crystallisation on plumage if these are not enclosed in polythene bags.

2. Paradichlorbenzene.

This is a very powerful volatile agent which has been extensively used for some years. It is, however, now regarded as responsible for undesirable colour changes in specimens. It is also believed, with prolonged exposure to its vapour, to involve a risk of lung cancer.

3. D.D.T. (dichloro-diphenyl-trichloroethane).

This substance is put up in spray form for domestic use and is an effective insect repellant and control agent. This spray can be added to, to protect specimens against mould, by the addition of one per cent. pentachlorphenol. It is cumulative and stored in fat in vertebrates, including man.

Comments: A highly toxic chemical, inhalation is to be avoided.

VIII. Materials:

Tow.

Wood-wool, fine.

Cotton-wool, absorbent and non-absorbent.

Galvanised wire, various gauges.

Wire-netting, half-inch mesh.

Balsa wood.

Hardwood sawdust.

Plaster of paris.

Silver, and sharp sand.

Powdered glass. Note: This substance looks *exactly like soft sugar*, and must therefore be carefully controlled, especially from children.

Carpenters' glue, and other adhesives.

Dextrin.

Pipeclay, powdered.

Light magnesium carbonate.

Potato flour.

Sand-paper, various grades.

Twine, thread and cottons.

Artists oil colours and brushes (assorted).

Turpentine.

Varnishes, copal and shellac.

Winton Retouching Varnish (Winsor and Newton, England).

Dry colours and distempers.

Glass eyes, various sizes, coloured and uncoloured (obtainable from natural history stores).

Papier-mâché.

Modelling wax.

Pastes.

Nails, screws, staples, assorted sizes.

Silver Fleece steel wool for glass cleaning.
Assortment of small pans and dishes (many uses).
Assortment of pins.
Tin or light aluminium foil.

IX. Personal Protection

Soap and water.
Plastic (disposable) gloves.
Plastic apron.

CHAPTER FOUR

MAINTENANCE OF A COLLECTION

NO one should contemplate forming a collection without accepting, at the very moment of commencing, the challenge offered by various contestants in the venture. The proper maintenance of a collection means contending with various animate and inanimate factors, all bent on destruction.

By far the most burdensome of these are certain species of small beetles (*Coleoptera*), and of these, those belonging to the genera *Anthrenus* and *Dermestes* are certainly the most damaging despoilers of our handiwork. Lesser culprits are the group known as " spider " beetles from their superficial resemblance to spiders ; the two species met with are the golden spider beetle (*Niptus hololeucus*) and the Australian spider beetle (*Ptinus tectus*), while the following must also be mentioned, the bread beetle, (*Stegobium panaceum*), the common furniture beetle (*Anobium punctatum*), the cigarette beetle (*Lassioderma serricorne*), and the two-spot carpet beetle (*Attagenus pellio*). The common furniture beetle, whose larva is the familiar " wood-worm," and various species of the genus *Lyctus* are prone to attack the cases in which mounted birds are displayed, though they do not attack the specimens themselves.

Three species of moths, the common clothes moth (*Tineola bisselliela*), the case-bearing moth (*Tinaea pellionella*) and the brown house or false clothes moth

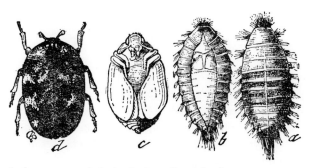

Anthrenus scrophulariæ (enlarged). a, b, larvæ ; c, pupa ; d, imago.

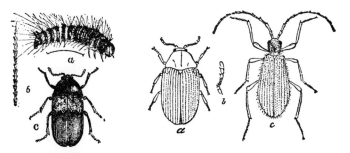

(Left) — *Dermestes lardarius* (enlarged). a, larva ; b, a magnified hair ; c, imago. (Centre) Bread beetle, *Sitodrepa panicea* (enlarged). a, imago ; b, magnified antenna. (Right) Spider beetle, *Ptinus brunneus*.

(Reproduced by courtesy of Macmillan & Co., London, from Elliott Coues' *Handbook of Field and General Ornithology*.)

(*Hofmannophila pseudospretella*) are also responsible for depredations.

What are the signs that any of these pests are at work ? Such are only too obvious and the visible damage of loose feathers, or a fine powdery dust must be immediately investigated.

The first line of defence is, of course, constant vigilance, for the damage is insidious and can proceed a long way before discovery. The second line is to house the collection in insect-proof containers. Skin collections should not only be contained in such but, as an added safeguard they should be put into polythene bags. A collection which is in frequent use is far less vulnerable than one that is stored. In this respect skins are easier to protect than mounted birds. The latter should receive a regular spraying with D.D.T., at least bi-annually. Display cases containing single or groups of birds need to be overhauled regularly and their sealings checked.

The above measures coupled with the use of an insect repellant should go a long way to controlling the evil. Specimens received from any source should be put into isolation until known to be free from hidden pests.

In public museums, sterilisation by heat is the method of choice, and by this means specimens are baked in an autoclave up to 212°F. or even higher, but if subjected to too high a temperature, singeing of the plumage will result.

Incidental damage, particularly of mounted birds has to be guarded against, and damp, dust and dirt are the environment beloved of the lowly little creatures we have been discussing ; disturbance they dislike intensely.

Finally, of course, use insect repellants; naphthalene is now regarded as the first choice, and a few flakes should be placed in the drawers of the cabinets. However, polythene bags should still be used as they protect from insects, dust, damp, damage and also afford some measure of protection against fading.

The other physical factor capable of ruining a collection is light, and this applies as much to a north light as to direct sunlight. Birds exposed to light will in the end fade beyond recognition, and they are, therefore, best accommodated in a blacked-out room, illuminated only as required by fluorescent daylight tubular lighting.

The above outlines the measures which should be taken to safeguard a collection, and these, if followed, should prove effective.

GLOSSARY

Abdominal, appertaining to the abdomen or belly.

Adrenals, small paired glands situated at the upper ends of the kidneys.

Anatomy, the study of the structure of an organism.

Articulation, a joint, space between two or more bones.

Autopsy, the examination of a dead body.

Axillaries, the long feathers growing from axilla or arm-pit.

Backbone-s, the bony spine.

Beak or bill, consists of the bony core and horny covering of the mouth parts of birds.

Breast-bone, strictly the sternum (q.v.).

Cadaver, corpse, dead body.

Carcass, see corpse.

Carpal-joint, wrist joint.

Carpus-al, the wrist, appertaining to the wrist.

Caudal, appertaining to the tail.

Cervical, appertaining to the neck.

Clavicle, see also collarbone, furcula and wish-bone. Fused into one piece in most birds, absent in some.

Cloaca, the terminal cavity of the intestine in birds which receives the bowel and urinary excretions, also the egg before it is laid in females.

" Cocky-hen," any female bird showing masculinisation.

Cocoon, a larval stage of many insects.

Collar-bone, see clavicle.

Cranial, appertaining to the cranium.

Cranium, that part of the skull containing the brain.

Crown, the top of the head.

Debridement, to trim the edges of an incision.

Digit, finger.

Digital, appertaining to the fingers.

Dimorphism, two different phases of the same species, or as sexual dimorphism in which the cock and hen are distinguishable.

Distal, the end of any structure beyond its attachment to or origin from the body.

Ear-coverts, the small feathers covering the apertures of the ears, in birds.

Eclipse plumage, a plumage assumed by the cocks of some species at the end of the nesting season in which they resemble the hens, best seen in various duck species.

Ecto-parasite, a parasite living on the exterior of a bird.

Endo-parasite, a parasite living within a bird's body.

Eviscerate, to remove the viscera of an organism.

Facies, face, the facial aspect.

Femur, femora, the thigh, thigh bones.

Fly, hippoboscid; bird-, cuckoo-fly; sluggish, flat flies living in the plumage.

Furcula, see clavicle.

Gape, the opening of the mouth.

Gonads, the sex glands, testes in the male, ovary-ies, in the female.

Gonys, that point on the mandible (q.v.) where the two sides meet.

Habitat, the chosen environment in which any particular species lives.

Hallux, the hind toe.

Heel, the joint situated immediately above a bird's foot, and directed backwards.

Henny-cock, a male individual showing signs of feminisation, see also Mule bird, and Intersex.

Humerus-i, the upper wing bone.

Hybrid, the progeny resulting from the cross of two different species.

Imp, the repairing of broken feather quills by wiring end to end.

Impervious, as applied to nostrils when septum separates the one from the other.

Integument, the skin.

Intersex, an individual of either sex showing characters normally found in the other.

Iris, the coloured part of the eye.

Joint, see Articulation.

Larva, an early stage in the metamorphosis of insects and some other organisms.

Loral, appertaining to the lores.

Lores, the space between the base of the bill and eyes.

Mallophaga, bird lice.

Mandible, the lower jaws.

Mantle, regionally the area of the back and scapulars.

Maxilla, the upper jaws.

Metacarpus, the remnants of the components of the hand.

Metamorphosis, the changing phases passed through by some organisms until the final form is assumed.

Metatarsus (anatomically), see Tarsus (ornithologically).

Microfilaria, the pre-larval stage of various species of thread-like worms in the blood of birds.

Moult, the shedding and renewal of feathers, and sometimes other structures.

Mule bird, see Intersex.

Nail, applicable to structure on bill or toes.

Naris-es, nostril-s.

Nostril-s, the apertures seen on the sides of the maxilla.

Oil gland, see Preen gland.

Orbit, the bony cavities housing the eyes.

Ornithology, the study cf birds.

Ovary, the organ (sometimes paired) containing the egg cells.

Oviduct, the tube down which the eggs travel ; secretes shell and colour.

Palate, the roof of the mouth.

Parasite, see Ecto-and Endo-parasite.

Pectoral, appertaining to the breast.

Pectoral girdle, the bones forming the shoulder joint.

Pelvis, the expansion of the backbone which gives attachment to the legs at the hip joints and the pygostyle (q.v.).

Pervious, applied to nostrils, lacking a septum, c.f. Impervious.

Phalanges, see digits.

Preen glands, the paired glands situated on the upper surface of the pygostyle (q.v.). See also Oil glands.

Primary sexual characters, see Gonads.

Proximal, nearer to the body, c.f. distal.

Pygostyle, the ultimate segment of the backbone.

Quill, the medial stem of a feather.

Radius, the slighter and thinner of the two bones of the forearm.

Rectrix-ices, tail feather-s.

Remex-iges, flight feather-s.

Rigor mortis, the phase of rigidity after death.

Scapula-ae, the shoulder blade-s.

Scapulars, the group of long feathers arising in the shoulder region on a bird's back.

Secondary sexual characters, all those characters distinguishing the sexes, excepting the testes in the male and ovary in the female.

Shoulder girdle, see Pectoral girdle.

Sperm ducts, the tubes conveying the male cells from the testes.

Sterile, incapable of reproduction.

Sternum, the breast-bone.

Tarso-metatarsus, see Metatarsus, Tarsus.

Tarsus, the scaly (sometimes feathered) segment of a bird's leg between the toes and the heel (q.v.).

Testis-es, see Gonads.

Ulna, the larger of the two bones of the forearm to which the secondary remiges are attached.

Ureters, the tubes carrying away the waste products from the kidneys.

Vent, the opening of the cloaca on the exterior.

Viscera, the internal organs.

Wish-bone, see Clavicle.

BIBLIOGRAPHY

DONOVAN, Edward. 1794. Instructions for collecting and preserving subjects of Natural History. London.

SWAINSON, William. 1840. The Cabinet Cyclopaedia, Taxidermy, Bibliography and Biography. London.

COUES, Elliott, M.A., M.D., etc. 1890. Handbook of Field and General Ornithology. London.

DAVIE, Oliver. 1894. Methods in the art of Taxidermy. Philadelphia.

SCHUFELDT, R. W., M.D. 1894. Scientific Taxidermy for Museums, Washington, U.S.A.

BROWNE, Montagu, F.G.S., F.Z.S., etc. 1896. Artistic and Scientific Taxidermy and Modelling. London.

HASLUCK, Paul N. 1901. Taxidermy. London.

GRANT, Claude H. B. 1914. The Shikari. A Hunter's Guide. Chapter 6. Taxidermy.

BRITISH MUSEUM (NATURAL HISTORY) London, 1921. Instructions for Collectors: No. 2—Birds and their Eggs.

DIDIER, R. and BOUDAREL A. 1921. L'art de la Taxidermie. Paris.

EYKMAN, C. 1949. Taxidermie S'—Gravenhage.

MOYER, John W. 1953. Practical Taxidermy. London.

PRAY, Leon L. 1956. Taxidermy. New York.

ANDERSON, Rudolph Martin. 1960. Methods of Collecting and Preserving Vertebrate Animals. National Museum of Canada, Bulletin No. 69. Biological Series No. 18.

HARRISON, James M. 1961. The New Wildfowler. Chapter 27. Wildfowl Taxidermy.

HARRISON, James M. 1961. The New Wildfowler. Hybridization in Wildfowl.

HARRISON, Jeffery G. 1961. The New Wildfowler. Wildfowl Viscera Removal.

INDEX